Verse-A-Tell-It

To my FB Friend
David Hammond.
Best Regards
Adrian "Ray" Evans
2-16

Verse-A-Tell-It

By

Adrian Ray Evans

Strategic Book Publishing and Rights Co.

Strategic Book Publishing & Rights Co. LLC
USA | Singapore
www.sbpra.com

For information about special discounts for bulk purchases, please contact Strategic Book Publishing and Rights Co. Special Sales, at bookorder@sbpra.net

ISBN: 978-1-68181-049-2

A special thanks to my nephews, NASCAR racing legends, Michael Waltrip and Darrell Waltrip, for their support in this book.

Additionally, I'd like to thank my nephew Joseph Eugene Hagan for the photographs of myself for this book. And a special thanks to my son Adrian Ray Evans Jr. for his continued support in my endeavors.

Educate me (with facts)

Don’t brainwash me (With trickery)!

(Adrian Ray Evans)

About the author

Adrian Ray Evans was born January 18th, 1934, on a rundown farm somewhere near West Louisville Kentucky. His father worked in a nearby coal mine and did a small amount of working the dirt-poor ground to raise food for the family.. His mother did all the house chores and raised four children.. Times were tough; beans was the primary meals.

Adrian Ray Evans was always known as 'Ray'.. His first name rarely came up until he joined the Navy in 1950. The father died of rectal cancer when Ray was eighteen months old.. The family was struggling, so the mother decided to give up two of her children to foster care to lighten the load and expenses.. Ray was one of them, at age two.. A couple of foster homes did not work out, until a lady took Ray to her farm near Birk City, Kentucky.. Birk City was a 'non spot' on the Davies County map, a few miles from Owensboro, KY. The farm was partially bounded by the Green River, where the foster parents fished with trot lines and nets, in addition to tending the 150-acre farm.

Ray would stay with this family for the next ten years.. The foster mother was controlling and in charge of all aspects of their lives.. The foster father rarely had any contact with Ray, so he never really knew a father figure. The foster mother hovered over and controlled Ray to a fault.. Although the farm was rather productive, money was short and luxuries were nonexistent.. The motto of "A penny saved is a penny earned" became an annoying repetition to Ray.

The farm was sold, and Ray and his foster family moved to Owensboro when Ray was in the sixth grade.

At 13, the 'much too old' foster parents decided Ray was too much for them and sent him back to his 'real' family.

His mother had now re-married and had three more children.. Both parents worked, and the kids pretty much run free.. The step-father directed all his attention to his own three children, and again Ray had no father figure. In fact, it was a tenuous relationship at best. It was difficult for the family to make it on the little money the parents earned.. At fourteen, Ray got a paper route for a while, then a job in a diner across the street from their upstairs home.. A 'little person' had purchased an old train car and converted it into a diner.. Ray was soon trusted with nearly running the place.

After convincing his mother to 'fib' for him and declare he was seventeen so he could join the Navy while he was still sixteen, Ray became the youngest-looking sailor in the Navy.. Folks sometimes thought he was in the sea scouts. Certainly no one in the Navy would be a father figure.. Ray had become used to being fatherless anyhow.

While stationed at a Naval Air Station north of Philadelphia, PA, Ray met and married a girl who later gave him six children.. In the meantime, he was honorably discharged after nearly four years in the Navy.

He had no high school diploma, and so civilian life was tough, so Ray studied and received his diploma through the GED program.. Then it was a sales job with an insurance company.. After that, a sales job at a radio station.. Alcohol became too much of a part of his life, which became a mess.

Then a truck driving job.. A divorce after about 25 years of marriage and then a downward spiral of alcoholism nearly killed him. Ray finally got his addiction under control.. He re-married and went into business for himself as a painting contractor.

Having a desire to help others with addictions, Adrian 'Ray' Evans' first book, *Woeful Wisdom*, told of the bad times of an alcoholic and his recovery. He writes about himself as a drunken alcoholic who ultimately became free of the disease's hold, and now has more than thirty years of sobriety.

In *Verse-A-Tell-It*. Mr. Evans imparts a great deal of his "eighty-some years" of wisdom and views to all who may care, about some facts of life, insights, whims, and plain old common sense.

He credits the 12 steps of recovery program that he has been participating in ever since he stopped drinking, December 1, 1983, for giving him the ability to live a better and a more productive life without the assistance of any mind-altering substances.

The range of subjects is provided in verse as it tells the story in the author's views; hence, the title *Verse-A-Tell-It*. Instead of chapters, the author chose to categorize the subjects in books, numbered from one to ten.

The range of subjects, some humorous and some very serious, has either been experienced personally or researched, and are not intended to have similarities to any persons, living or dead, except where noted.

Author Adrian Ray Evans
Photo by Joseph Eugene Hagan

by Adrian Ray Evans
Available on Kindle and in print and
at most book stores, Amazon and
through Outskirts Press at.
outskirtspress.com/woefulwisdom

Stolen from the internet:

An old farmer had owned a large farm for several years. He had a large pond in the back forty, had it fixed up nice; picnic tables, horseshoe courts, basketball court, etc. The pond was fixed for swimming when it was built.

One evening the old farmer decided to go down to the pond as he hadn't been there for a while and look it over. As he neared the pond, he heard voices shouting and laughing with glee. As he came closer he saw it was a bunch of young women skinny-dipping in his pond. He made the women aware of his presence and they all went to the deep end of the pond.

One of the women shouted to him, "We're not coming out until you leave!" The old man replied, "I didn't come down here to watch you ladies swim or make you get out of the pond, I only came to feed my alligators."

Old age and treachery will triumph over youth and skill every time!

(Author unknown)

PREFACE

THE OCCASION BOOKS

This here is the occasion books; inside here is where you look

To see how I rode out the bumps and dings, and get my views on different things.

I thought if my book was all in rhyme, it might best stand the test of time.

In these pages you'll find laughter.. Or could be advice is what you're after?

Concerning advice, I'm not real smart, but what I say, comes from the heart.

Those who know me very well, know that lies I don't tell.

From alley to mansion, white collar to hard hat, I've been there; I've done that.

Being rich and famous was my destiny, but along the way, something happened to me.

Kinda' got caught up in a rut; spent too much time sittin' on my butt.

On too many barstools I got sicker, thinking the answer was in hard liquor.

Then one day, I got real smart and to a higher power, I opened up my heart.

I listened to what folks had to say as they 'fessed up, around AA.

Now my sober years are over thirty, my walk is straight and very sturdy.

With my conscience, I'm peacefully livin'.. For I know, I've been forgiven.

My serenity is in its wealth, for I finally forgave myself.

My first book was WOEFUL WISDOM, it told of my drunken prison.

In this edition, I see a whole new look, that's why I call it the Occasion Books.

DEDICATIONS

TO MY WIFE JO ANN

I wrote this poem on October 8, 1987, to my
'then' girlfriend, Jo Ann.
We were later married on March 10, 1988

One great day I'll own Times Square, I'll be a multi-millionaire.

I'll be captain of all the seas, be the force of a gentle breeze.

I'll fly a rocket ship; I'll build a boat, around a castle I'll dig a moat.

I'll climb all heights that temp my sole all things I touch will turn to gold.

No evil or devil will there ever be, either in or out or beside of me.

The clouds will be mine to touch and caress, the sky will shroud me, with gentleness.

My Garden of Eden will be completely filled, as I know 'my God' has gracefully willed.

At least in my heart, that's how it will be, the day my Jo Ann goes down the aisle with me.

A special thanks to my nephews, NASCAR racing legends, Michael Waltrip and Darrell Waltrip for their support in this book.

Michael Waltrip – (through his rep) "MW said he's all good for you to use his name in your book. Said he's glad to help"!!—

Darrell Waltrip (about this book) "I like it, you always had a way with words! Glad you found a place to express how you feel! Love you". DW.

Additionally, I'd like to thank my nephew Joseph Eugene Hagan for the photographs of myself for this book. And a special thanks to my son Adrian Ray Evans Jr. for his continued support in my endeavors.

BOOK #1 The way it was

BOOK #2 Roots

BOOK #3 Inspirations

BOOK #4 Passionate Race fans

BOOK #5 Holidays

BOOK #6 Weather

BOOK #7 Bad Guys

BOOK #8 Romance

BOOK #9 Seniors

BOOK #10 Fond farewells

I – Z – THE END

Biography

Adrian Ray Evans was born in a farmhouse in Western Kentucky during the Great Depression.. A recovering alcoholic, since December 1983, he is retired from his own house-painting business (Adrian Custom House Painters) of Orlando, Florida, where he lived and worked for forty years.

After his retirement, Mr. Evans and his wife returned to his hometown, Owensboro, Kentucky, in 2012 to be near ailing family members and to spend the remaining years of their lives.

Mr. Evans still uses his brush to please and beautify the world with his oil paintings, creating landscapes, seascapes, stills, and abstracts under the pseudonym "Arts by Adrian R.". Primarily a self- taught artist, Mr. Evans attended only a few organized art classes.

Several of his paintings have won ribbons. One of his abstract paintings has received wide acclaim, depicting the attack on the World Trade Center.. He entitled it "EVIL" as a response to President George Bush's labeling of the attackers as "evil".. At this printing, Mr. Evans has completed over 500 paintings, some of which can be "liked" on FacebBook under the name Adrian Ray Evans.

A veteran of the U.S. Navy, Mr. Evans served during the Korean Conflict in the early 1950's as a radio operator aboard the USS Fessenden, DER 142.. The Fessenden was a WW2 Destroyer Escort, converted into a radar picket ship for the

Korean War, patrolling a portion of the US eastern north Atlantic shores. After Korea, it was scuttled in Pearl Harbor Bay to be an artificial reef.

Woeful Wisdom (Outskirts Press) was Mr. Evans' first book, which was intended to help other alcoholics by telling about his own experiences and recovery.

In this book, *Verse-A-Tell-It*, Adrian Evans is also the artist who painted the art work illustrated in this book.

A REAL FUN RIDE

In this book you'll get the score, a real fun ride is what you're in-for.
As I sit down at my writer, my mind fleets like a midnight rider.
It skips hither, thither and yon, until it finds a phrase to land upon.
As if down from the sky, the words come into my mind's eye.

I go real fast at each key, so from me the thoughts don't flee.
I do a line and then some thought; keep up the pace that I've brought.
Try not to forget how I started; from my theme I can't be parted.
I must remember the goal in mind is to tell a story and make it rhyme.

I'd like to pass along some worthy wit and be true while doing it.
A laugh or two, here and there, a little smarts and a little flair.
I may not rite really well; I don't even know how to spell.
But I have messages from my heart; important stuff to impart.

The only way I know to share is to type away without a care.
If it's proper text or proper writin' just as long as it's excitin'
To the ear I hope to please, as I bang on computer keys.
The end line should be worth reachin', no four letter words... and without preachin'.

So tighten your belt and set your phone aside, these books will take you on a real fun ride.

BOOK ONE

The way it was

MORNING AFTER

DEAR MOM

To my dear Mom I'd like to say things I didn't before she passed away.

I was so wrapped up in my selfish me; she was a gem I failed to see.

At my birth, she was so poor; she had to give me to the lady next door.

And away from Mom I did roam, with that lady in her foster home.

It was hard for her to part with her Son, but she did what had to be done.

There were still others left to feed and she was still bound to meet their need.

Her energy did not diminish old furnishings she would refinish.

She'd make quilts for the bed, and stuff feathers in a feather bed.

I grew distant and rarely did see, the sweet Mom that gave birth to me.

Over the years, I did come to visit, but not long enough for love to get with it.

Then my life, it went astray, going further down most every day.

I was so busy bringing shame to all of those who shared my name.

I lived near Mom on some short stays, She was not happy with my sinful ways.

She'd fuss at me for the life I'd built, so I'd move away to hide my guilt.

I'd seek out a geographic cure, why it never worked, I couldn't be sure.

Then it loomed up in front of me, wherever I went, I took me with me.

Then the well know straw that breaks ones back, the one that hits hard, and doesn't slack.

Came when Mom died and left this world, my fake cover, did unfurl.

I was far away, down and out, all I could do, was drink and pout.

I missed Mom's funeral and what a shame, with another stone I slammed my name.

Then I knew, it was time for a change, my personal life I needed to re-arrange.

I sought help and will power too, started to build my life anew.

Now if my Mom's spirit could really see what her death has done for me.

From the booze I now abstain, so her end was not in vain.

"I love you" was not said to her at all, not even once do I recall.

From me those words were never spoken, no gesture of love, not even a token.

It's sad to me I just never saw, the true love inside my Maw.

So with this verse I say to you, "My dear Mom, I do love you."

GRANNIE'S HOBBY

MOM'S TABLE

START ANEW

I am one of the lucky few, who got a chance to start anew.

My life has changed which I don't regret, from whence I came, I won't forget.

There is still a soul or two, who won't accept the 'me' that's new.

For those of you who can't consciously, accept my utmost apology.

I understand and you're not to blame, you may still think I'm playing a game.

You stay so far away, you see, you haven't met the real new me.

Your lack of interest in my being, the real new me you're not seeing.

The one you once did abhor is not that one anymore.

My childish ways and social affliction was being fueled by my addiction.

That was not me that you knew then, I lacked the stuff to be with men.

For many years I've done my penance, I've served out my just sentence.

My page has turned my leaf is new and my inner being just grew and grew.

With serenity I'm surrounded; with clear conscience I'm abounded.

I had to step up with nerves so fearless, just to give myself forgiveness.

Judgment is passed on most my cases; I've been forgiven in higher places.

So for those, who are so few, that can't see the me that's new.

You live your life and I'll live mine, perhaps we'll meet in a future time.

You'll forgive me and I'll forgive you, we'll love each other and start anew.

TRUST

I can speak of trust, in life it is a must.

Once there was no trusting me, for I was far too blind to see.

A word that is unkept makes one so inept.

Inept at being human, unable to be a new-man.

I once dwelled on selfish things, now I know what that fault brings.

I'd not give you a single thought, as my word was worth a naught.

My credit could not stand up, money and morals were all bankrupt.

Then I saw the light, hope loomed up in my sight.

I jumped on morality, folks found a trust in me.

Trust has come my way, and now is here to stay.

I feel a great accession; trust is my new possession.

If there's no trust in you, it means you are untrue.

Keep your word and credit safe; you'll then live in a happy place.

You will find that it's a must to have and hold a moral trust.

FAITH OF MY OWN

Without a faith of my own, I roamed the streets all alone.
I was homeless as a child, un-kept and running wild.
I appeared as a hopeless kid, down through the cracks I always slid.
My young years knew no faith; there was no God in my space.
So in my youth I would pause, and ask for things from Santa Claus.
But Santa Claus I only saw in a window at the mall.
Then a stranger appeared to me; said come my son, I'll set you free.
Into a mission we did go, in the warm away from snow.
Soup and bread I was fed, and a place to lay my head.
I did not stir nor did I panic, when that stranger he did vanish.
Whoever he might be, a lot of hope he gave to me.
That I would bloom just like a flower, and find for me a higher power.
That Santa was a stepping stone while I sought faith of my own.

COTTON TOP

When I was a boy, my hair was soft and white; it stood out in the bright sunlight.

My mom thought I was really cute, and dressed me in a funny suit.

I had plenty hair for comb-n' and primp-n'; my mom thought it was really sump'n.

My face got red and my ears did pop, when they called me cotton-top.

Old ladies would finger my cute curls, and I got stares from little girls.

The boys would laugh and stick out their tongues, I would scream at the top of my lungs.

It was mean the way they did, it made me feel like a real strange kid.

In the words of a farmer I had a full crop; that's why they called me cotton top.

As a teen I'd had enough so I used a lot of that greasy kid's stuff.

I flattened the curls and dulled the whiteness, in the sun there was no brightness.

I even got a short crew-cut but my hair was so soft, it wouldn't stand up.

I tried a hat but someone said it would cut off the blood to the top of my head.

Make me stay short and not grow tall, my head would get mighty bald.

As the years came rolling round, my hair went from white to blond to brown.

That's when the girls began to notice me; I was as popular as a guy could be.

Now I'm old my head is slick and shiny, with no hair, just like my hinny.

My entire head is one bald spot; they no longer call me cotton-top.

TREE HOUSE

As a little boy, my heart was filled with great joy
When my dad built for me… a house up in a tree.
It had a walkway on a slope and a ladder made of rope,
A lounge chair and TV; he put up there, just for me.
My table and my bunk were not made of back yard junk;
Quality did abound, high up off that solid ground.
The sides were neat and very trim, out upon a sturdy limb.
Dad gave me some field glasses, to peer out through the tree branches.
Happiness was meant to be, in my house up in a tree.
Then I awoke, and things got bad, I realized I had no Dad.
There was no house up in a tree; I had dreamed a fantasy.
I awoke in a shelter tent, cold and hungry and without a cent.
I was hit with brutality, no Mom no Dad, no family.
Then a lady came from nowhere, said for me, that she did care.
A foster parent was her role, into her world I would go.

I'd be clothed, fed, and sent to school and learn the live by the golden rule.
This life with her and her spouse was much better than my tree house.

DARE

As a kid I didn't have a prayer because of those kids that would dare.

They'd dare to do this and dare to do that, and then double dog dare me to combat.

It was their way of child trickery to get me involved in their tom-foolery.

A fool of me it would often make, because their stupid dare I'd sometimes take.

They'd dare me to go real real high, or off a cliff they'd dare me to fly.

They often did it and thought it was right; they would dare me to join in their plight.

A dare from here and a dare from there, I was getting dares from everywhere.

I'd climb a tree way too high then couldn't get down, so I'd cry.

I'd jump a ditch filled with water, all along knowing I shouldn't outta.

If my school clothes I got wet, my little behind would pay the debt.

Foster Mom was strict, strict as could be; she kept me hidden from reality.

I wasn't talented or aware and such; I was caught in an apron string rut.

With other kids I couldn't keep pace, for me it was a three legged race.

Now that I'm older and doing social media, all caught up in face book mania.

I hesitate when I get a call, to re-post something upon my wall.

On my neck it raises hair; it comes across as another dare.

I feel I'm being tricked don't you see, 'cause it stirs up an old memory.

My mind can see you giving me the test, crossed arms across your chest.

Upon your neck your chin you force, from under your brow your eyes are coarse.

All you're doing is daring me, to re-post this so other will see.

Whether it is Politics, or religion, if you don't mind, I'll make my own decision.

With your message I might agree, but that should be left up to me.

Now I'm big and I don't care, you can't move me with your dare.

ONE NATION - 48 x 60 oil on gallery wrap board.
Depicts the USS Fessenden, DER 142, the author's duty ship in the early fifties.

ONE NATION (under God)
No matter what a person's beliefs, in my opinion
the tradition of
'Under God' should always remain.

I WAS A SAILOR

(Veterans Day Salute)

I was a sailor in U.S. Navy sailing the ocean, deep and wavy.

Just a kid, didn't need to shave, but I was proud and felt really brave.

My friends thought I was crazy for signing up with the U.S. Navy.

But I was a kid and didn't have a girl; it sounded like fun to sail around the world.

Oh man, did I get a big surprise, that tough man's Navy, opened up my eyes.

They said make your bunk and march at dawn, you're a man now; you're on your own.

I said what? I'm just a kid... I wanted to do what all kids did.

To sail around this pretty world, and in every port have a girl.

They said "Oh no, you don't get it son, you're not here just for fun."

When you're wearing that coat of blue, here are some things you must do;

Stand tall and straight and very proud, be a gentleman in any crowd.

Swab the deck and wash those dishes, forget all about your childish wishes.

You're a man now, that's for real; you're sailing around on a ship of steel.

Be ready to fight other ships at sea, just be sure they are the en-a-mee.

Don't turn and run back to the rear if that ship is from North Korea.

We'll hold our water, 'stead of our ground, while we're out here sailing around.

We are Americans and we try harder, to prevent another sad Pearl Harbor.

By keeping our country safe and free and be proud for being in the U.S. Navy.

SLUMS

Waking up in the slums somewhere… being drunk and lying there.

One helluv place to lay and crash, in a puddle of puke, among the trash.

Clothes all wrinkled and out of sorts, smells like a mess, in my shorts.

One shoe missing and the other ragged; why did I fall off that damn wagon?

I've gone beyond a simple blooper, wound up in a drunken stupor.

Can't remember how long it's been, since I got in this awful spin.

Must've started a while ago… back about a month or so.

My sobriety I did pitch, wound up here, in this ditch.

Beside a road that goes nowhere, in this terrible slum somewhere.

I see bugs and I see vermin; in my skin I am squirmin'.

I hope this is the worst it gets.. I'm having those horrid, D.T. fits.

If I survive this terrible deal, I'll quit drinking, that's for real.

But I've heard me say that before. How many times have I swore,

I'd quit this stuff and start a new life, be true and faithful to my wife.

Be a real Dad to my kids no more of these rotten skids.

Show that I really care, not wake up in a slum somewhere.

I've heard there's help along the way with a famous group called AA

I'll admit that I am smitten, this damn booze I am a- quittin'.

I'll take the pledge and stand up there; tell my story of despair.

Take my life out of the glum's,. keep my butt out of the slums.

DUMPSTER TRUCK

I once did pick up trash; I'd pick up trash from the street.
I'd revere that trash with affection; I guess I thought it was so sweet.
I've picked up rotten tomatoes, and now I must admit,
I've picked up trash from a trailer park, and made passionate love to it.
    I've picked up trash on the highway, when I would see a thumb out.
    Then I'd take that trash with me, to a nearby trashy hangout.
    I've done things wrong when I picked up trash in a roadside park,
    I never knew what that trash was, when we got trashy in the dark
Now something strange has happened to me, now my 'me' is re-arranged.
The light came shining through, my life has really changed.
Where I once took my trash to bed, now I take it to a can instead.
I am smarter now but not yet a scholar, the trash I now pick up, is so much smaller.
    I don't seek trashy as a love; I don't seek comfort from a Bimbo,

I don't spread trash on the street; I don't throw it out a window.
I carry a poop bag with me, every time I walk my Rover.
Let me tell you friend, my trashy days are over.
The real smart thing for us, is take care what we do,
I've often heard about some things that will come back to you.
I got a job in a trailer park, and don't you know it's just my luck,
That job turned out to be a job, driving a trashy dumpster truck.

BOOK TWO

Roots

BLESSED TIMES

LITTLE OWENSBORO

A tribute to Owensboro Kentucky.
(My home town)

Ole little town of Owens-boro
Smack on the banks of the great Ohio.
Where the water turns in a bend,
Where love of life, never ends.
Home of the big blue bridge;
A real neat park at the water's edge;
We don't have slickers, from the city;
Our farmer's daughters are mighty pretty.
We have churches and we have steeples,
Our neighbors are the friendliest peoples.
We have malls and we have shops;
Our welcome wagon is the tops.
Other things I could mention,
like that new center of convention.
Where top entertainment will be a thrill,
brought directly from Nashville.
So don't wake with sorrow tomorrow,
Do not miss our little Owens-boro.

RADIO COUNTRY

Some Radio announcers have a lot to say between the tunes that they play.

They yak and yak and talk commercial; some are bad without rehearsal.

Then there are others who go by the script, their top bosses demanding it.

Now some will play three tunes or more before they announce to you the score.

The tunes have titles, but they won't name 'em. They think we have our radio game-on.

We sit there with our hands a wringing trying to guess the one that's singing.

Then if they do give us the drift; it's way at the end of their playing shift.

The worst of all is the morning bunches, blabbing away till noon lunches.

Three or more will talk at once, the radio speaker you want to punch.

You scan the dial through static and whispers, searching for a station coming in crisper.

Then you find it and yell out bluntly; whoop-de-doo, I found some country.

Lots of pickin' and lots of singin', foot stompin' sounds and tambourines jinglin'.

You know you've found the best of all when you hear yodel and nasal drawl.

The radio announcer will stay pretty quiet, if he doesn't, there may be a riot.

He will keep us up to speed on only the info that we need

To enjoy our country music pleasure and know the facts about the stars we treasure.

Now and then a little radio add; but not enough to make us mad.

I will say it and say it humbly, nothing can beat our Radio Country.

TV COMMERCIALS

We're watching TV and we hit a snag.. Here comes a commercial to nag, nag, nag.

We can turn down the volume or mute the set, but those commercials to us will get.

I hear we need-'em to pay the fare, of a TV pro-gram on the air.

We've paid for the TV and the elect-ter-ris-ity, and the satellite service ain't for free.

We pay for the guide that lists the stuff, let's tell them greeds we've had e-nuff.

And the commercials they do lie, about the junk they want us to buy.

They use phrases that sound delicious to sell things that are suspicious.

They twist a line and sound it sharp, but when we buy, it falls apart.

They don't care if you keep it or not, as long as our money in their pocket they got.

Most commercials leave me wishin'.. I'd left the TV and gone fishin'.

Let's stop my cussing and fussing and stewin', just take away the commercials from my viewin'.

So who's gonna' pay that lost fare, let's do it the same as OBAMACARE!

YOU SHOULDN'T DRIVE IT

Back in the early fifties, we drove autos that were not real nifty.
We were poor, our cars were sore; we couldn't afford a fix-em store.
When something broke, a garage was a joke,
So we used spit and bailing wire, and rode around on four bald tires.
Now times have changed, roads are re-arranged,
Don't depend on luck, or you'll get real stuck.
The rules are now more strict, breaking them will get you ticked.
So here's some stuff I'm gonna' offer, to keep you safe and fill your coffer.
Before leaving in your car, remember you need to click it.
If your car belt doesn't work then you shouldn't drive it.
Did you use you turn signal when you turned that corner?
Does your signal just not work or did you pull a boner?
If your signal does not work it's up to you to fix it.
If it was a small mistake, it's time for you to nix it.
If you're changing travel lanes, but don't show your plans,
you for sure will be taking, your life into your hands.
If you zoom through a light 'cause it's changing red,
You and someone else could end up dead.

If you don't wait your turn at that there four way stop,
You may be facing more than just an angry cop.
    Darting in and out and driving way too fast,
    will anger other drivers and put you in a body cast.
    Driving up too close to someone's trunk,
    can turn both your cars, into auto junk.
Saying that you didn't know will never ever solve it.
If you're ignorant of our laws,
or if your car has some flaws,
then you shouldn't drive it.

A FURNISHED HOME

A big difference from the fifties

I went a-car huntin' the other day; things just didn't go my way.

The prices are so outta' whack, the price of a Kia is more than a Cadillac.

Inflation is not the only cul-prit, the stuff they add makes you wanna' spit.

I bought a house back in nineteen sixty; that little cottage was mighty nifty.

The total cost I had to pay, was one quarter of a car today.

The house I bought was unfurnished, and the extra cost did not punish.

We added a TV and a stereo, soft leather seats and a radio.

We put in carpets, wall to wall, and a phone for us to call.

Window shades and glass that was tinted, and our air, it was scented.

Air conditioned and heated too; all that stuff was real brand new.

If you give it some thought, you will say, all that stuff is in a car today.

So if you could buy that car unfurnished, your budget would not get so punished.

When ole Henry invented the four spooked wheels, he didn't expect the furnishings in the deals.

So in your small car as you roam, you're ridin' around in a furnished home.

PAINTER POEM

Thoughts from when I was a house painter

LITTLE PEOPLE PAINTER

Once there was a painter who dabbled on houses and such.
He'd splash on paint with a big bristly brutch.
He'd climb up a ladder to the peak of your adobe.
And paint your treasure into a happy mode.
Then dash inside with a mischievous grin.
And paint all the walls there within.

He'd make you cheerful and happy to pay.
For all the nice work he'd do that day.
Just one thing that bothered him so greatly,
was climbing on mansions so high and stately.
A fear of heights was his waterloo,
Climbing up and getting down too.
He'd breathe deep as he left the ground,
not look up, or not look down.
But with assurance from high above,
he knew his angel was watching with love.
He'd mutter to himself so quietly,
"You need some help, from psychiatry!"
"Get down off this ladder, you silly schmuck."
But you don't get down off a ladder,
You get down off a duck!

WHEELS OF CHROME

. . . From my truck driving experiences

Eighteen wheels of chrome, rollin' west, away from home.
Eighteen wheels and eighteen tires… haulin' heavy loads for big money buyers.
Dropping some here, and dropping some there, everything's dropped with special care.
Dropping and picking up, is what one does in a long-haul truck.
Gliding along in an air ride seat… slab road seams, keeping a beat.
Country music wafting through a good sound system; a deer jumps out, just barely missed-em.
In my big rear view mirror, a jet black Beemer is getting nearer.
On the left as they pass by, two blonds with skirts hiked up high.
They smile and wave and toot their horn, then up the road they are gone.
Made me think of what I just left 'way back home in my love nest.
Soft red lips and long brown hair, the love of my life is waiting there.
Up the road near the underpass, a sneaky cop parked in the grass.

His radar pointed out the side; if you're speeding, he'll have your hide.

In the next town, there's a scale for weighin'; as I approach, I'm softly sayin',

"Hope all my papers are up to date and my truck ain't overweight."

Stop for fuel in Chattanooga, then over Mt. Eagle and hallelujah.

I made it down that crazy hill, didn't lose my brakes and did not spill.

At the bottom, thru fog I'm plowin'; better stop soon for some truck stop chowin'.

Nashville down to Memphis and on through to Texas; nearly got ran into by a guy drivin' a Lexus.

I can rest somewhat cheaper by snoozin' in my truck's sleeper.

I can dream so soft and sweet, in the bed behind my air ride seat.

When I deliver at my Texas connection, I'll hope for a re-load in an eastern direction,

back to my home in the east, to have a hot home cooked feast.

I'll sleep better in my soft warm bed with that long brown hair by my head.

I'll be glad I didn't stray or wander, when that Beemer passed me way back yonder.

I'm so glad to be in my home, brought back here on these wheels of chrome.

BOOK THREE

Inspiration

JUNIORS SUNSET

DANCE LIKE NO ONE'S WATCHING

Luck on your door is quietly knocking, so dance like no one's watching.
Stretch, yawn, and view the morning sun; it's a good day, for healthy fun.
The night has swept away, the troubles of yesterday.
A fortune of happiness does await, for those who have dropped, all their hate.
    Allow this day to rise and shine, your heart will feel, so divine.
    Like a Bunny hopping, dance, like no one's watching.
    Say "Hi" to strangers on the street, have a smile for all you meet.
    Forgive those who have wronged you, build yourself a brand new you.
And forgive yourself as well, on mistakes you mustn't dwell.
Take pride in deeds you have done, a new day, has just begun.
Your world is now unlocking so dance like no one's watching.

ACTION – REACTION

For every action there's a reaction, for every number there's a fraction.

Love and hate are close neighbors; lemon and lime are different flavors.

Black and white is much mistaken; the thought they're colors, should be forsaken.

White is a lack of any color; black is a mixture of all the other.

A distinctive color, they just ain't; remember that if you paint.

Forget square one, you can't start there; the circle of life is not a square.

What goes around must come back 'cause life is a rounding circle track.

Remember that wherever you're goin' 'cause you will reap what you've been sowin'.

It may not be just right away; later on it will come into play.

It doesn't matter about your religion; faults come back like a homing pigeon.

So if you're painting your life's path, don't leave behind a lot of wrath.

But if you make a mistake or two, forgive yourself and they'll forgive you.

Turn to the ones you may have hurt, an apology will often work.

In re-action to your action, you'll get a large satisfaction.

FEAR

Fear to a lot of us is no stranger. It's a distressing emotion of impeding danger.

A practice that in we delve, a lack of faith in ourselves.

A larger than life paranoia; larger than a huge Sequoia.

Fear places restrictions on our lives, can cut deeper than sharp knives.

Fear can leave an open and hurtful wound. We can feel lost and forever doomed.

But fear can be replaced with eternal hope to give us strength and power to cope.

Turn it around to be a motivator, raise us up like an elevator.

Give ourselves a reason to cheer;

Kick the crap out of fear.

NOT COLOR DID I SEE

Not color did I see, for me that was strange, as seeing color, is really my thing.

Because I'm an artist and I love the hues, of the reds, yellows, greens and blues.

But this one day colors were blind to me, because a little hand-up, was all I could see.

A man walking along the side of the road, a can of gas he carried as a hefty load.

I stopped and offered him a ride, which he accepted, swallowing his pride.

His strange look as he kept staring at me, as tho I had done something so heavenly.

He asked what I had in mind, by picking him up, was I color blind?

His strange question had taken me aback, but it was because me being white and him being black.

An explanation was easy for me; it was someone in need, not color did I see.

I FELL UPON A TREE

As I stumbled through the woods so dense, my mind was living in the gone past-tense.

So consumed was I in yesteryear, my path ahead was not so clear.

The vision of eyes and the sense of nose were wafted away with dwelling on woes.

Indulging and salivating in an old misery, of gone happenings that should be his-to-ry.

Was I here to fish or hunt, or was my back getting ahead of my front?

My solitude was all broken into by ancient thoughts that make me blue.

Then I tripped and fell upon a tree, it was lying there dead in front of me.

It was all dried and somewhat rotted, and all over its bark, green moss I spotted.

It once stood stately, sixty feet or so, but that must have been a long while ago.

Now there it lay in the path of hikers and me; that once tall, proud and glorious tree.

It did its dues in the circle of life, making no waves and causing no strife.

With beauty and shade and buffeting the wind, to all who passed by, just being a friend.

Now here its leafless trunk does lie, blocking the way of passersby,
Or maybe not as I think of it, now I see a chance to sit.
I can slow my pace and gaze at the sky, and let the woods' beauty fill my eye.
Not think of the things that were bad, but reflect on all the good times I've had.
So this old tree is still not dead; it gives a place to clear my head.
If In death, like this old tree, I too could useful be,
I'd be glad I fell upon this tree.

HOLE IN MY SHOE

When I was a kid, we were poor, hand-me-downs was our décor.

Sometimes rags, but never riches, I always had holes in my britches.

Rich kids don't know how it feels to share baloney at most their meals.

Eggs and bacon were rarely seen; sometimes our bread looked kinda' green.

Sometimes a potato would grace our plate; if you wanted some, better not be late.

But we were healthy and didn't care, we never wore dirty underwear.

Our house was neat and our bodies were clean. Soap was bought as well as beans.

Our minds were free of dirty thoughts. The golden rule was what was taught.

Be kind to each other and love thy neighbor, don't be afraid of daily labor.

Just one thing gave me the blues; I had holes in the bottom of my shoes.

The soles were loose and would flip-flop; the strings were ragged and tied in knots.

There was no money for shoes this year.. Kids would make fun, stare and jeer.

Now I'm old and about to go and having a problem with my center toe.

The old arteries are clogged and the blood is slow, can't get enough to the center toe.

"Cut a hole in the shoe." is what the Doctor said. "And the toe will heal and won't stay red."

So that's exactly what I did. Made me think of when I was a kid.

Instead of holes in the bottom and soles that go flip-flop, I'm ashamed of the holes I cut in the top.

PATIENTS

Patience is a virtue; patience you should nurture.

Having lots and lots of patience can benefit your future.

If you lose your patience no one will help you find it.

If your nerve gets all wound up, patients will help unwind it.

Don't always be in a rush; in a line don't shove or push.

If you're waiting for a meet, be real calm and keep your seat.

Jumping up and pacing too… will not do a thing for you.

Don't send your patience down a hill; let that baby come at will.

If you're waiting for a plane, read a book-- don't go insane.

Don't press yourself to be adult, be slow to give your childhood up.

Don't wish away your time so precious by wishing the future to soon be with us.

Getting promoted can be a dread; don't step on toes to get ahead.

Don't take the road of least resistance; buckle up and keep your distance.

You'll be surprised how fast you'll go, while being calm and going slow.

Don't give way to bad impatience, hold your ground and be real patient.

I HAD A PLAN TODAY

I had a plan today,
Whatever it was, it went away.
Now I'm stuck, in a rut,
an empty feeling in my gut.
How did I manage to lose myself?. It's not like me,
I'm usually very happy you see.
Was it the nightmare in my tossing sleep?
Or the dream in which I had no feet?
Going back to bed would be a good decision,
getting up on the other side, with a different vision.
Yet another way to add my day with flare,
Would be to repeat to me… my Serenity Prayer.

MIRROR MIRROR

Did I look in my mirror without restraint?. Look deep into me, the not-so-saint?

Did I have fun at someone else's expense? Did I annoy or make someone tense?

Did I use some generous soul, to make me feel big, brave and bold?

Did I lie to some fellow man, just to make my ego feel super grand?

Did I make up stories to paint pretty me, or did I settle for what I'm meant to be?

Did I work to improve me instead of the other guy?

If I didn't, please tell me why.

Did I lose my spirituality, through the use of vulgarity?

Did I see the beauty in my midst, or did I slander with maliciousness?

Did I lose it momentarily? But then man up and take responsibility?

Did I hurt someone today? I'm pretty sure I didn't, because I'm not that way.

Did I ask you mirror, to keep me narrow and straight?

Don't let a hateful soul be my fate.

Did I look from your glass with serenity?

Knowing tomorrow I could look again with honesty?

FACE BOOK HUBBY

I'm a retired flunky, a face book junkie, my nieces and nephews say I'm their best Unkie.

My friends would like to see me more but I'm locked up behind my man cave door.

I keep peckin' away at these stupid keys; my pears I'm trying so hard to please.

My kids think I'm a real gone daddy, a good candidate for a wagon called paddy.

But folks like my art and stuff, and no one yet has cried…"dat's enough!"

So I'll just keep on playin' with this here 'puter.. I'm too old to find anyone cuter.

I'll spend my day in a face book haze, too damn dumb to change my ways.

Sittin' on my butt, gettin' fat and chubby, the wife's on the couch –

without her face book hubby.

ELECTION DAY BLUES

All over TV, paper and radio too, enough about elections to make us feel blue.

How can we trust anything they say?. Once in office their plans go away.

Is anything we hear really true?. Could they be fooling folks, like me and you?

The money they spend on all that baloney is more than the check of a rich alimony.

And most of that is donated by a few of us, just to hear them throw each other under the bus.

If the other guy is a fake and can't be trusted, it's just plain sense, they all need busted.

Can't they see the picture they paint? That honesty among them, well it just ain't.

They start out rich and get even richer, and the mud they sling gets even thicker.

They smile and wave and con us as well.. Don't they know they're on their way to Hell?

Well, maybe not 'cause we're stupid, we praise their names as though they're Cupid.

An arrow and a bow they do not tote.. The only love they have is for the vote.

We vote for this one and that one too.. Hoping when they win, they'll all be true.

Our world doesn't get better or up to snuff. When are we gonna' say, we've had enough?

Don't vote for those who can't be true.. Let's vote in a monkey or two.

SMOKING

Smoking, smoking, I once did it, and then I tried hard just to quit it.
It never once occurred to me, what a chore that would be.
I'd throw away my cigarettes, and I'd be hoping,
if I had no cigarettes, that I'd soon quit smoking.
    A mess it made of me, my nerves came unraveled.
    I'd whine and whine like a child and up the wall I traveled.
    I chewed up gum and bit my nails; my train of life went off its rails.
    I did patches and I did pills, they were to cure my smoking ills.
But all I did was get sadder, without a smoke, I got madder.
To those days there was no ends, I lost my temper and my friends,
Then I saw the light one day, I threw those dang pills away.
I really got my gumption goin' that damned habit I need throwin'.
    Don't rely on phooey stuff, set your mind not to puff.
    I faced the facts and admitted to it, I said "its work, but I can do it."

Now I'm smoke free and sure am glad, the smell of smoke ain't in my pad.
There's lots of money I save each day, since I threw those butts away.
I'm often asked "how'd you do it?" and I reply "there's nothing to it."
I said "look here Dude, smoking's nasty and it's rude!"
If you really want to quit, my little secret I'll share it;
I stopped fighting it every day; I used the twelve steps of AA.

FAT TO FAT

Wherever I go, on land or sea, my belly gets there just ahead of me.

I wanna lose weight but I just keep eatin', I go ona diet but then start cheetin'.

'Stead of chompin' th calories, I need to chomp th bit, but just can't seem to put my mind to it

It's so damn hard to just say no, to cakes and pies and fattenin' dough.

There are sodas, ice cream, delicious candy, all sorts of stuff that's super dandy.

I could eat and eat till I pop, just never know when to stop.

To get away from all that goo, I've heard it said all I need to do,

Is use will power when that hunger bell rings, gotta say no to many many things.

Turn to veggies and lettuce and stuff, but that sounds so dang tough.

But if a rabbit can do it, so can I, I'll eat carrots to the day I die.

I'll much on cabbage and turnip greens; I'll be a veggie blending machine.

Eat a little less when I sit to dine, take in the belt and trim the waste line.

Get off my butt and take a walk, a little more action and a little less talk.

I'll do some squats and then a chin up, run around the gym like a feisty pup.

Pushups at the gym and push-a-ways from the table, someday I'll be thin like a fiber optic cable.

I'll turn my face away from naught; the only food I'll chew is food for thought.

I'll grow wiser and thinner as well, on eatin and gorgin I won't dwell.

Dust to dust and fat to fat, eatin' too much ain't where it's at.

I'll give up sweets one after another, all except my significant other.

MOVE

Don't let your feet be of lead, one needs to move to get ahead.

Move on up when in school, study hard, don't be a fool.

Move outa' the way if someone's speedin', or a doctor you'll be a needin'.

If you wanna' move up that ladder, do things in your job, which really matter.

If you're moving across this great land, it's much easier, in a moving van.

Move your body and do some workin', to keep your health, and stay good lookin'.

So moving things is good for you, to keep you happy and healthy too.

There are other ways to do improvin', keeping friends and your character movin'.

I don't have a medical degree, but to me, it's plain to see,

for no strikes, no errors, and no fouls, go to the John and move your bowls.

Heed this wisdom that I impart, and there'll be less stink -- when you fart.

BOOK FOUR

Passionate race fans

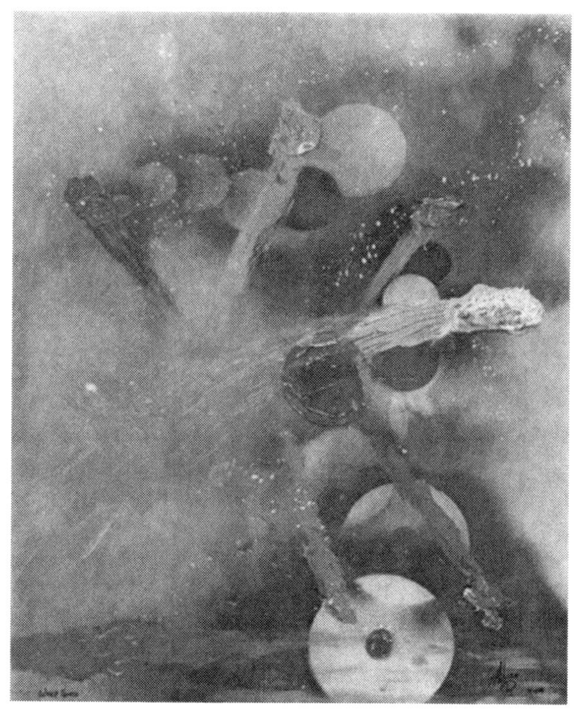

WARP SPEED

STAR ATHLETE

If a race car racer isn't running number one, that race car racer isn't having much fun.

They aren't just racing for the fun of it, they're also racing for the money they git.

Not to mention the kudos and high praise; the adrenalin and the blood pressure raise.

Driving the machine they call KARZ; going real fast on four new TARZ.

Those words stem from an old tradition, when drivers were south of the Mason-Dixon.

They ran fast on a back road, and White lightin' was their payload.

When the revenuers found their stills, twas to the race track they turned their skills.

They put on helmets and an innocent look, and tried to live by a NASCAR book.

For some of them, that was mighty tough.. Making an honest living just wasn't enough,

They needed excitement and feel the chase, so racing took the moon shine's place.

They competed against each other; farmer against farmer and brother against brother.

Now it wasn't the cops on their heels, it was another driver on four wheels.

Around the track they would go; you got run over if you were too slow.

They turned to sponsors for the money they's a needin', to pay the toll of their zest for speedin'.

They painted their cars to look real pretty, sometimes dull, sometimes witty.

The sponsor was the one to choose, the designs and stripes and all the hues.

But it was the drivers and their machines that took the chances and the flags of green.

They were backed by a brave pit crew, that stuck right there 'till the checker flew.

The winners circle would hold just one, so the rest of them just run for fun.

Car racing started with some system abusers, illegally selling to sots and boozers.

Now they're legal and a proud sort. Everyone knows that car racing's a sport.

A driver that once was dirt under the revenuer's feet is now considered a star athlete.

A NASCAR CAR

A racing fan will travel far, to hear and see a NASCAR car.

A NASCAR car doesn't have mud flaps; they don't even have shiny hub caps.

A NASCAR car is a buddy; if it's run through the grass, it gets all muddy.

But stay on the track like you should, and a NASCAR car will treat you good.

They're not built for highway runnin', they're all painted up to look real stunnin'.

Don't take those paint jobs very lightly, the bright bold colors show us brightly,

Their sponsor's name and logo pretty, and some text to sound real witty,

That body is welded to a special need, the supped up engine is tooled for speed.

There's a special chair in the cockpit, a real hot seat for the driver to sit.

A real big mirror for a special view to watch the one that is chasing you.

A net on the window, you can feel wind blowin'; and a roll cage for crashin' and a rollin'.

Four on the floor that's rarin' to go. 'Ya get bumped in the rear if you start to slow.

A tough bumper that'll send you crashin' if you don't move when someone's passin'.

High octane is the racing fuel; save some for the end, that's the rule.

Four new tires that are speed slick; savin' that rubber is a crafty trick.

Oversized brakes that get fiery hot if you push 'em.... quite a lot.

To save rubber, fuel and brakes, a lot of patience is what it takes.

Until it comes to the end, use 'em all up... and go for the win.

The crowd will love you and you'll go far, when you drive a NASCAR car.

RACING ANALYZERS

If you are a NASCAR fan, this stuff here you'll understand.

It's about cars that go round and round, hit the wall and turn upside down.

Its cars that starts two by two's. It's about folks that hate to lose.

They push their gasoline pedal, to the car's floorboard metal.

They pass each other with a bump. If you don't move, your rear they'll hump.

The score is kept electronically; if you're down a lap, all can see.

Its dog eat dog on that round track; the lucky dog gets his lap back.

As the cars go pass the stands, you hear the cheers from the fans.

The TV cameras keep on a shootin', showing the action and the rootie-toot-tootin'.

The announcers get all excited, when a flipped car is up-righted.

They worry much about a driver; wanting them to be a survivor.

They interpret to the racing fans, technical stuff so we'll understand.

They paint a picture so we can see whatever we missed on TV.

They tell us when drivers are fools, or when one doesn't play by the rules.

They praise the drivers that are grand, and pity those who've been dealt a bad hand.

They're just as fair as fair can be, while giving us the racing his-to-ry.

They keep us informed and up to date; all the announcers, they are great.

Analyze the race is what they do; Make it very clear to me and you.

So instead of announcers and broadcasters, let's all call them racing analyzers.

RACING NIGHT

A tribute to the 4th of July race at Daytona, FL.

On the Fourth of July it's a big race day, in Daytona Florida, U. S. A.

The NASCAR boys all get in a huff, they've raced half a year, that ain't-e- nuff.

They've pumped up their TARS, and shined their KARS, you'd think they were racin' for shiny gold bars.

But monetary gain is only part of the show; they're racing for fame as round they go.

Celebrating the spirit of seventy six while racing for their NASCAR fix.

They scrape and scratch any car that's near, and even bump 'em from the rear.

So pick your favorite NASCAR drivers; stand up, yell and be an idolizer.

Wear their shirts and buy their hats, you-th-fan is where it's at.

Without you, my fast car friend, NASCAR racing would come to an end.

Now hop in your wheels and don't forget to click-it, fight the traffic and buy a ticket.

Take your spouse and your spouse's mother, if you ain't spoused up, take your lover.

Wave a flag or a pennant; show the world you're really in it.

The best car goes to the circle of winnin', with its driver who won't stop grinnin'.

Ya better not miss that racing night, the post race fireworks are a sight.

You'll drive home with a heart that's light, having enjoyed your racing night.

AN ODE TO MICHAEL WALTRIP

A tribute to my nephew Michael Waltrip,
NASCAR, driver/Team owner

Michael also appeared on Dancing with the Stars in 2014.

Mi-keee, Mi-keee,. Mi-keee, a celebrity you will always be.

You shined with the stars, dancing up there in all your glory.

But from a racing fan here's the story;

Your dancing puts the judges at a loss, go back to Daytona where you are the boss.

Calling a race or making a face, hittin' the wall with amazing grace.

Passing this one and passing that one, round and round in a circle of fun.

On the track or in the garage, you're quick with a talking barrage.

Where most of us wouldn't have a clue, you're at home with a 'mike and a camera too!

Your smile is contagious; your humor is outrageous.

From the track you should never leave us;

So don't go twisting and shaking your legga; we like you better at Talladega.

DW SAID

(Another tribute to my other racing nephew, Darrell Waltrip)

D. W. said… "BOOGITY, BOOGITY, BOOGITY", and "let's go racing boys."

To get the cars started racing, and making lots of noise.

He has a way of exciting and getting one stirred up; He makes you want to follow NASCAR's racing cup.

When he becomes reactive, our funny bone gets active,
but he can be serious and quite matter-of-factive.

Ole DW, I really like him best when about a blunder, he can jest.

One day a wheel went off and flew over the wall, ole DW chimed in, didn't miss a call.

He sang "you picked a fine time to leave me, loose wheel."

We thought of Kenney Rogers and his hit song, "Lucille."

When three cars are racing hard; each they're trying to kill, he hasn't said it yet, but I bet he will,

"Double your pleasure and double your fun. Try racing with two cars 'stead-o-just one."

He's a three time champ on the racing circuit; now he's on TV, he knows how to work it.

But an ole country boy he still is; heel kicking the ground and drawling "Aw Gee-Whizz."

He'll praise the Lord and quote a phrase right from the book of holy ways.

He's earned his stuff and deserves his joy.. I can say that, 'cuz I knew him as a boy.

He's my sister's son; that makes us kin, some say he and I, have the same kinda' grin.

I'm so glad we're related and a Waltrip my sister dated.

Now if you wanna' know the meaning of Extraordinary,
look under Darrell Waltrip, in your dictionary.

BOOK FIVE

Holidays

THE SEASON

CHRISTMAS AT HALLOWEEN

I saw Christmas lights on Halloween, and they weren't the colors that make you scream.

They were reds, yellows and blues, and variations of different hues.

Front yard trees were trimmed up bright. But for Halloween it just wasn't right.

Some folks had just jumped the gun, and messed up our Halloween fun.

They just couldn't seem to wait for December to celebrate.

The traditions of our Christmas cheer, the most joyous time of our year.

Christmas ads were boldly seen, starting back at Halloween.

Some skipped over the Indians giving to us the meaning of thankful living.

Except for feast and belts crammed tightly, Thanksgiving Day was taken way too lightly.

The stores opened up to sell their wares, families had to work, but stores didn't care.

Turkey leftovers were put away, and wits were being sharpened for Black Fri-day.

But by now Christmas ads weren't new, they'd already been seen a time or two.

The charity bells were already ringing, on radio stations carols were singing.

Oh yes we'd stolen all the delight, of the joy of Christmas Eve night.

Trees were up waaay too early; patience had grown just a bit surly.

The advertising time had too many days, to get our money in greedy ways.

And when we thought our spending was through, we thought of another gift or two.

Now you know, the reason is green, why they start Christmas at Halloween.

A TURKEY NAMED JANE

Thanksgiving was a bit away, so I planned ahead for that special day.

I bought a turkey when it was young, penned it out back and up it sprung.

It ate and ate till it got stuffy, it grew big and its feathers got fluffy.

There were times I could hardly wait, to see that bird on my plate.

I could picture a drumstick and a wing or two; my hunger was growing as that gobbler grew.

My wife would pet it and gave it a name, why on earth would she call it Jane?

My wife and Jane, they often played, in the pen out back where Jane stayed.

Jane thought my wife was her mother.. They would chatter and gobble to each other.

I knew it would be tough when Jane's time came, my bird loving-wife wouldn't be the same.

I got out the axe to do the deed, and there was wife, giving Jane some seed.

I said "Wife, you gotta' step aside. I want this Turkey with dressing inside."

The wife said "No" and wouldn't budge "If you hurt my Jane, I'll carry a grudge"

"I'll hate your heartless and killing hide, I'm gonna' save this turkey" is what she cried.

So what on earth was I gonna' do?

For Thanksgiving dinner, we had Tofu...

A CHRISTMAS WISH OF SOBRIETY

A poem I wrote on Dec 19, 1984, one year after I quit drinking and turned my life around.

I wish I were a Santa Claus, with a sleigh so huge and sleek.
Loaded down with so-bri-e-ty, to pass thru every street.
I'd pass it out here and there and everywhere, and all around you bet.
And everyone who wanted it, their share they'd surely get.
I'd give it to the young and old, and all those in between.
I'd give it to the good and bad, and even to the mean.
And man would I be rich when I got my dues, for giving all that
so-bri-e-ty to you and you and you.
And if I were a Christmas saint, I'd pray a lot for sure,
for all those poor dreadful ones, who haven't found the cure.
I'd give thanks to my Higher Power upon grateful knees,
that I'm not out there still, drinking poison squeeze.
Since I can't be those great and wondrous things,
put me at the front of the pack, pulling on the reins.

Put a red bulb in my nose, and call me little deer,
I'll be the leader of the pack that's spreading Christmas Cheer.
And I'll guide my Santa's Sleigh, down thru the halls of AA.
Carrying the big book all the way.

Merry Christmas to all.

HOLIDAY HAPPY

I'm wishing for all to be holiday happy; every son, daughter, maw and pappy'

I didn't leave CHRIST outta' our MAS, to exclude the holy living.

I said HOLIDAYS, to include all three days: New Year, Christmas and Thanksgiving.

Different beliefs have their different ways, which each are entitled to pursue.

Freedom of religion is our right, and by George, it's their right too.

Don't be picky over something sticky, tomato or tamahto, potato or patahto,

Let's praise with all just like we ought to.

Peace on earth, good will to men no matter which country you're living in.

If your Christmas is just another day, may you always have it that way.

Let's all rejoice and not be crappy, spread our love and be holiday happy.

SANTA'S CHIMNEYS

'Twas the night before Christmas, and all through the house,

I was stirring in socks and stepped on a mouse.

The mouse did squeak, my wife did shriek,

And Santa fell from the chimney with soot on his cheek.

He was dusty and black, from his head to his sack.

He was not jolly or friendly at all; it seems someone forgot to clean the chimney last fall.

Well, Santa is a real forgiving guy, so he left the toys and returned to the sky.

Back home at the North Pole.. Back with his spouse and out of the cold.

While shivering and hugging dear Mrs. Claus, and the reindeer were licking the snow from their paws,

He summed up his weary night, he told her of his dusty flight,

to which she said "I have a solution my dear." "If they don't clean their chimneys,

Stay home next year!"

OLE GIFT CARRIER

Christmas is a happy time, and a time for yulein'.
Christmas cakes and pies; and little people droolin'.
Christmas carols a singin', Sally bells a ringin'.
Snowflakes lightly fallin' and Santa's sleigh is haulin',
love and gifts wrapped in paper, and special shoes for the skater.
A robe for the Dads, and gifts for the grads.
A special gift for mothers, sisters and their brothers.
All sorts of stuff that's neat, In back of Santa's seat.
Those reindeer are not a foolin', they love the load they're pullin'.
They are told to dash away, and dash away they do,
through a snowy sky, a snowy sky of blue.
Through each and every neighborhood, to every kid that has been good.
He flies past geese a flockin', to fill every Christmas stockin'.
On radar he's a blip; no good chimney does he skip.
No place on earth will he ever miss, leaving love, gifts and Christmas bliss.
And when he's done with his Christmas role, He'll fly back to that northern pole.

The elves will greet him with applause, a kiss he'll get from Mrs. Claus,
And the entire world will be merrier, because of this jolly ole gift carrier.

NEW YEAR'S DAY

It's a New Year's kind of day; I've often heard it said,
what I do on this day will be done in days ahead.
So I said to me, as I took down the Christmas tree,
I think I'll meditate; on my future I'll concentrate.
Wipe my mind of thoughts so sad; whisk away the times so bad.
Aha that was easy do, cause bad times, were so few.
Now I'll lay my brain to task, counting up the good I asked,
Thankful for the answers given and I'm still among the livin'.
The year before I now can see wasn't all that bad for me,
And the year that's coming up will completely fill my cup.
If there not be an eye that's dry, joyfulness will be the why.
I'll steer away from self pity, keep my troubles itty-bitty.
Welcome, welcome New Year's Day, sure am glad you came my way.

RESCUE-LUTIONS

It's New Year's Day, I'm gonna' re-adjust, doing what's right to keep up trust.

Some will call them resolutions, but to save my mind, it's RESCUE-lutions.

A bad image I don't create, there's just some things to re-iterate.

I just want to make it clear, about some things I hold dear.

To save my body from dreadful fate, I promise not to stay up late.

It's early to bed and early to rise, my great day, I won't compromise.

I'll do my best to get real fit, to dance and sing, because of it.

I'll not pick at things what're bad, I'll dwell on the good times I have had.

I won't grumble, I won't complain, even if the day has been a strain.

I won't say things that hurt real deep, I won't make promises I can't keep.

I won't work up a useless lather, over small stuff that doesn't matter.

I'll really listen when someone speak, not to my phone will I peek.

I'll not interrupt till they stop speakin', our 'get-along' I won't weaken.

About my day I'll not dramatize, won't make up stories, I won't tell lies.

I won't feed my ego; I won't see red, starting when I get outta' bed.

I know full well what's to be done, just face the world and don't dare run.

I'm the one to cause bad stuff; I must resolve I've had enough.

There are lots of things I need to see, in order to rescue me-from-me,

For me, there's a positive solution: don't forget my RESCUE-lutions.

THANK YOU

My birthday was a real big happy, lot of good wishes to take away my crappy.

Now I'm singing and playing my air guitar as I ride around in my car.

I got cards and wishes galore from the west and eastern shore.

My kids and family they're so nice some even wished me happy birthday twice.

From my Nieces and Nephews too they see to it that my blues are few.

And on my birthday they think I'm special, their wishes remove stuff that's so stressful.

My screen filled up with a birthday look from all my friends on my Face Book.

So from the bottom of my heart to you my thanks I will impart.

Now I can announce the very latest, thank you, thank you; you're the greatest.

ARROW, ARROW

(Make her mine)

Arrow, Arrow, please go straight, into the one I want to date.

That's the pretty one over there; the one who has the curly blond hair.

Eyes of blue and cheeks so pinkish, a little smile that's so impish.

The one with rosy on her lips and polished stuff on her finger tips.

She could be the belle of the ball, while I'm the weed on the wall.

She can't see me and I know why, 'cause she's beside another guy.

Arrow, go straight into her heart, so she and I can have a start.

Get rid of the jerk there by her side; I think I want her for my bride.

Give me the gift of speaking smooth, so in my arms, she will move.

Give us love and true affection, get us started in the right direction.

Do for us what arrows do, melt her heart and let us woo.

Just she and I for all time:. Arrow, Arrow make her mine.

BOOK SIX

Weather

HURRICANE HAPPENING

COLD WEATHER

This weather is so alarming, when th heck will it start warming?
Further south, I should really go. The cold is driving me, oh so nut-so.
They talk about the freezing, the coughing and the wheezing.
The flue is getting rampant.. They're trying hard to stamp-it.
The old shot isn't working, 'cause a new strain there is lurking.
If the temp's not cold enough, the wind-chill makes it tough.
I don't like this here cold, the wind and rain is getting old.
The snow will sometimes skitter, upon the lawn it does litter.
I need a heat reliever, I'm getting cabin fever
Big blankets on my bed, a sock-top on my head.
My P-J's are of flannel. I need a solar panel.
The north wind's getting bolder, my toes are getting colder.
Fingers are getting numb, outlook's very glum.
I should reverse my thinking, get rid of thoughts so stinking.

Let my tears be dried,.. look to the brighter side.

Think to the months ahead when winter will be dead.

The birds and bees will gently swarm, and sunny days that will be warm.

We will all sing songs together, and forget about this dang cold weather.

COUGH 'N SNEEZE

(To the tune of 'Jingle Bells')

Cough 'n sneeze, cough 'n sneeze, a cold from Christmas day

Cough 'n sneeze, Cough 'n sneeze, can't go out and play.

A day or two ago, went to Grandma's place.

The roads were snowy white, the wind froze my face.

I sat by the fire to see if I could thaw,

Hot tea I was served, brewed by my Grandma.

A big sneeze did escape; Blew food off my plate

into the waiting lap. of our cousin Kate.

Oh… cough 'n sneeze cough 'n sneese…. a cold from Christmas day

Cough 'n sneeze… cough 'n sneeze…. I'll be sick till New Year's Day.

Ole KY.

Cold weather to me is not so pleasing; my fingers and toes, they are a freezin.
The frost gets to my ears 'cause I lived in Florida for a number of years.
My blood is much much thinner, in cold weather I'm just not a winner.
My feet get numb, my hands get rough, I'm just not very winter tough.
My throat gets sore; my nose goes sneezin', my lungs get chilled and starts me to wheezin'.
    The brittle bones in my back get so cold, they nearly crack.
    The knee joints are really very tight and the elbows hurt me in the night.
    If I could, I'd leave my home and return to where the gators roam.
    I'd fight the 'skeeters and roaches too If I could go back to Orlandu.
I'd hit the beaches at Daytona and breathe in deep the salt aroma.
I'll feed the sea birds from my hand as I picnic in the sand.
I'd pick up sea shells and eat oranges, beautiful Florida is where my heart is.

But my home is here in Kentucky, so I guess I'm really lucky.
I've got a wife that warms me up, with her flowing loving cup.
A bunch of new friends to make my day, give me strength and show me the way.
I must be here for another reason, than to fight the cold cold season.
So I'll do no more of the movin scheemin, and rely on my dreamin.
If I dream of Florida, I might cry, so I'll be happy in ole K. Y.

SNOWSTORM #1

It's the 2015 storms of snow, reminds me of a storm so long ago.

I was somewhat younger and not too wise; it took years to open my eyes.

I had to learn to deal with the cold and such; sometimes for me it was too much.

Now this is a story of how it went, way back when I was a younger gent.

I looked outside and saw all snow. The door was clogged, out I could not go.

I climbed out through a window, trying to be a hero, fell on my butt and wound up a zero.

My strong will power I sure did thank, as I dug my way out of that snow bank,

But I had to use my hands don't you know, to dig my way outta' that there snow.

The ole snow shovel was buried deep, next to the door in snow and sleet.

When I did finally get a hold of it, I was so tired I had to sit.

I really should have known, sittin on ice my butt wouldn't condone.

So I dug a tunnel to the door, slid in the house and fell on the floor.

The wife looked down at me and said, if you do that again, you'll wind up dead.

Said she in words softly spoken, "what good did it do to get th door open?"

"Both our cars are buried in snow, there's no place that we can go."

We're stuck right here in this snow storm, let's snuggle together to keep us warm.

That's what we did and when spring came, she told me I'd be a father again.

SNOWSTORM #2

I slid out the drive and spun around twice, everything was covered in snow and ice.

My four wheel drive just wanted to spin; I was headed back where I'd just been.

Then my conscience wuz tawkin' to me, just how dumb can one fool be?

A four wheel drive is good in snow, but on ice the four wheels won't go.

Four wheels on ice, thick or thin, four wheels will just four wheel spin.

And even if you have a four by four, do not push that pedal to the floor.

Don't hit the brake with a real hard push, touch it lightly and do not rush.

Take it easy and go real slo, or you might never go no MO!

If you really must go out in this, be sure to give your loved ones a byebye kiss.

You just might never see them again, because you didn't use your pea sized brain.

You had to be real real dense, and refused to use your common sense.

You failed to see the future distress, and went out in this horrible mess.

Makes one wonder in past tense, how do you teach - common sense?

SNOWSTORM #3

I've lived in Florida and I know for sure, through a storm for you to endure,

you must prepare and look ahead, stock up on pills and liquid meds.

Did you stock up on foods and stuff, are you sure you bought enough?

When I lived in Florida we had a reason, to be prepared for the hurricane season.

Snow or hurricane storms here's what you otta, store up lots of bottled water,

A storm is a storm whether it be cold or hot, if you don't prepare you'll be distraught.

In case the power lines do get broke, have some spare stuff you can evoke

Some dry ice for things that spoil, and a heater that heats with oil'

Batteries for your flashlight, candles for emergency light.

In case it last for days or weeks, be prepared to sit on your cheeks.

Store up some books and games to play, Or old old pictures to display.

Be prepared to busy your brain, or you just might go real insane.

Storm planning ahead is what we all should do, but for everything, isn't that true?

BOOK SEVEN

Bad Guys

EVIL

SOCIOPATH

A sociopath is a person with a psychopathic personality, whose behavior is antisocial, often criminal, and who lacks a sense of moral responsibility or social conscience.

His manners are that of a Neanderthal, but he thinks he's best of all.
He holds his fork like a primitive beast; his hat stays on while he eats.
He has no social principle, his actions are nearly criminal.
His words are always gruff, he brags of being tough.
His little deeds he flaunts; he'll bore you with his vaunts.
His workaholic deeds and ways, he boasts with shameful praise.
He'll do little bits of good, around his neighborhood.
His motives aren't complicated; he wants you obligated.
He'll prey upon your blunder; he wants to steal your thunder.
He can undo your stuff, about what you did muff.
He thinks one is weak, if we turn the other cheek.
What he doesn't know; a higher road we'll go
That we're being careful, not to sink to his low level.
Nothing gives you wrath, like a pesky sociopath.

NARCISSISM

Narcissism - Inordinate fascination with oneself:. Excessive self-love: Vanity.

A Narcissist is a dreadful bore; a social scab, a mental sore.

A self proliferation, a vulgar praising without foundation.

Forsaking friends, sisters and brothers to love oneself as no other.

A me, me, me way of thinking, that reeks with air that's really stinking.

A selfish mind that has one track, a twisted arm that pats one's back.

A broken mirror that sees just one, a sharing image is not done.

A narcissist will portray to you, most all things in fascist view.

They will test your sanity, with their exploded vanity.

They'll interrupt your conversation, to exploit their situation

They will not give the benefit, of your wisdom or your wit.

They'll tag you with a view that's dim, so that they will always win.

They'll never let you have your word; a narcissist is a dirty bird.

BULLY

Nobody likes this oversized dude. He is ugly, mean, and stupid rude.

Can we picture him, well let us try; but this dang picture will make you cry.

He isn't as big as in tall, but his waist is wall to wall.

His hands are small, and ugly stubby, his face is always a bit grubby.

He is always sad, his breath is bad, and he must've been an unhappy Lad.

Nobody likes him and he knows it; if he ever gets a friend, he always blows it.

He has no happy praises to sing; he can't rise above a single thing.

So he gives it all his best, to make all others feel unrest.

He is cold as a low crawling lizard; instead of a heart he has a gizzard.

A book he leaves on the dusty shelf, his favorite subject, is himself.

Behind your back, he will slide; this ugly bully has no pride.

He never talks well about anyone; being mean and nasty is his fun.

Loud and tough threats are his fantasy, because he's chicken as chicken can be.

He blows smoke like a choo-choo train; his muscles are small, just like his brain.

Like all bullies, tall, round or small, a nasty bully will have a ball,

Scaring you and making threats, but that's about as tough as he gets.

Stand your ground, and look real mean; he'll holler cop in a girlie scream.

Don't let 'em get away with it; Jump right up and make 'em quit.

Stand your ground and get in his face, put that bully in his place.

PAYBACK

Pay-back, pay-back, watch what you do

Whatever it is, it had better be true.

If you do false to another one, your pay-back won't be fun.

Be real kind in public places, or get slapped on one of your faces.

You have two faces; maybe even more, it just depends on what you're conniving for.

What I'm told and do believe, you only have misery up your sleeve.

There's an ego where your heart should be, and it needs feeding constantly.

You can't see past your Pinocchio nose, and out of your mouth vulgarity flows.

You've flipped your lid and flipped us off; your attitude is never soft.

Now I'm a forgiving sort of guy, but you I can't stand and I've told you why.

Forgiving you is gonna' be tough, but I'll do it when I've had enough.

Enough pay-back to balance the scales, and make up for your outrageous tales.

Someday I'll give you some slack, after you've gotten a BIG pay-back.

A LIAR

A liar is a person that can't be trusted; they can lie to you and not get busted.

They're so good at what they do; they can toy and walk over you.

They don't have a conscience or remorse; they're sneakier than a Trojan horse.

A liar is worse than a thief; but both of them will cause you grief.

A thief will take your jewelry, and a liar will steal your dignity.

Worming their way into your heart and tearing your whole world wide apart.

No sorrow for what they do; a liar can make a wreck of you.

If you weigh the loss and all the grief; a real good liar is worse than a thief.

Even praying to a power that's higher, you can lock from a thief but not from a liar.

TRUTH

The truth is such a sacred thing, love or hate, it can bring.

Is the truth coming from the heart: Or just the lips as they part?

Is the truth you speak, being fruitful; or being cruel and downright brutal?

Do you want to spread real love; or just your opinion do you shove?

Though the words you speak are real true, did you think of the meaning that comes through?

Could you have changed them and be more discrete, and make that truth be more complete.

Did you insist on advice really un-needed, just to get your ego firmly seated?

All those changes you suggested, were they needed or un-requested?

When you helped someone do their inventory, did you later claim all the glory?

Of their honor, were you being a leffert? Were you a thief of someone's effort?

The basic truth, did you edit, just so you could get the credit,

Were you really being helpful; or stealing thunder from someone successful?

When you helped someone with a task, in return, a big favor did you ask?

When someone else you do asses, is it fruitful or cause more stress?

Are you honest, or do you fudge, when someone else you try to judge?

I've heard it said and I agree, the well known truth will set you free.

A LIAR YOU ARE

You lie with such a straight face.. You lie so often, I can't keep pace.

You lied to me, and I remember it still. I do not lie, but for you I will.

I'll lie about my pocket money, just so you won't ask to borrow any.

I'll lie about how tired I am, so doing your work I won't get scammed.

I'll lie about losing my voice, so talking to you won't be a choice.

If it will keep you from yackin' a lot, I'll lie about how well I'm not.

I'll lie to you about where I am, just so you won't be coming around.

I'll lie today and make amends tomorrow, hoping my lying won't bring me sorrow.

I'm not lying right now, don't you see, 'cause lying is not the thing for me.

The truth is here under my skin, I'm fully aware that lying is a sin.

A lie will get you trouble further, one lie can only lead to another.

No one believes the things you say, I don't want to be seen, in that way.

You can never be a shining star; everyone knows what a liar you are.

DEVIL

When you make amends does it count the Devil?. You made his deal and got down on his level.

So does he owe you or you owe him?. The chances of amends are mighty slim.

Slim to nothing, as the saying goes.. The devil doesn't pay the debts he owes.

Did you use him, or did he use you?. Is the deal you made now overdue?

Did you swap your soul for unearned gain?. Dealing with the devil is real inane.

That old devil, he isn't your friend; with selfish gain, he's out to win.

He will make things easy to do, but the pay back will break you in too.

Your nerves will shatter; your pride will go.. That's the devils pay back don't you know.

Material things are not his favor; he wants to see your resistance waver.

It's the soul that Satin's after, he wants you in Hell for ever after.

He'll take back double for his trouble, and your trouble will be triple double.

He won't let you go no matter what you do;.. for the rest of your life he'll torture you.

Rise above his bad level.. Say goodbye to the rotten devil.

WHAT YOU'RE DOIN

You need to think of what you're doin;
A close love you may ruin.
  Could be wrath you will reap if you keep up your stubborn streak.
  Your hard head you need to soften; don't say no so damn often.
Don't upset the family tree;
Being honest is the best policy.
  A loving relation will go astray if you insist on having your way.
  For the cruel words you may have said, say you're sorry and hang your head.
Then regroup and get a new start;
Keep your loved ones in your heart.
  The proverbial bullet you need to bite;
  Just chomp down with all your might.
Don't just bite but do some chewin';
you'll need to change what you're doin'.

BOOK EIGHT

Romance

LEVITATION

BATCHLORHOOD

Got a little hunger, down in my tummy; go to the fridge and get sump'n yummy.

I open the fridge and what do I see, a bunch of green mold lookin' back at me.

This was when I'd be so sad; back when I lived in a bachelor's pad.

The place was messy and very un-kept; the floor was rarely ever swept.

The windows were bare without a curtain; I needed a mate, that's for certain.

But I was picky, oh so picky; finding a mate would be real tricky.

Because 'my' way I'd always been given, I liked that about bachelor livin'.

If I wanted to go, I up and went; it was my money and it I spent.

I didn't have to beg and plead to buy something I didn't need.

I would laugh and think it a joke if by Thursday I wound up broke.

I didn't take life very seriously; I was single and liked being free.

I dated gals and thought it was great until I met my present mate.

She stole my heart and turned my head so on my knees I humbly plead.

I ask for her hand in wedded bliss and then we sealed it with a kiss.

Now I'm feeling so high and mighty my money and house is so tidy.

I'm not broke and the house ain't messy, and on Sundays we go dressy.

I'm no longer a hopeless slob; I now have a full time job.

This married life, it's a fit; bachelor hood, I'm over it.

JO ANN

I'm a Jo Ann. Kinda' dope
    My Jo Ann gives me lots of hope.
I can't let my Jo Ann ever leave,
    I'd go into a Jo Ann kinda' grieve.
I feel so lonesome, when she's away,
    It's a Jo Ann, kind of day.
She'll be here soon, I surely hope,
    Guess I'm a Jo Ann, kind of dope.
There's only one Jo in my world,
    Guess I'm in a Jo kind of whirl.
Where oh where did my heart go wrong,
    To let Jo Ann in, where she doesn't belong?
I was doing so well by myself,
    Then came Jo Ann, that impish elf.
She twisted my mind and knotted my gut.
    And put me in a Jo Ann, kind of rut.
Now I'm married and have lots of hope
    I'm so glad I'm a 'Jo Ann kinda' dope.

LADY ASTRONAUT

(I wrote this poem in the early space exploring days of the fifties. It was my vision of future women in space.)

My Baby's gone on an overnight trip,
  gone to the moon in a rocket ship.
If you think I'm wrong, I'll tell 'ya what,
  I married a Lady Astronaut.
She zooms off here, she zooms off there.
  She's always zooming off everywhere.
A week or so ago, she went to Mars.
  She brought back a ship full of candy bars.
Now it's off to Venus, oh what'll I do?
  She might come back minus an arm or two.
She has courage, that I can't deny,
  There's not a thing that woman won't try.
She did her nails and powdered her face,
  while taking a walk in outer space.
But if you want my advice, then it you've got.
  Don't ever marry a lady astronaut.
She'll leave you at home alone and blue,
  While she zooms around the earth in an orbit or two.
You'll get long letters from the government
  They don't ask if she can go, they just say she went.

Now you've heard my tale of sorrow and woe.
But there's one thing you all should know.
Though I'm alone with the beans in the pot I still love my lady astronaut.

FOOTBALL GAME

The person I am now is one and the same, as the one you met at the football game,

The one with whose attention you flirted, and my life's path you diverted.

Was it really meant to be; a football game, then you and me?

We dated a while then became lovers, a wedding ring and under the covers.

We went too fast that's for sure. Now we think divorce is the cure.

I couldn't change you and you couldn't change me; we're the same people we were meant to be.

The person I am now is one and the same as the one you met at the football game.

Why can't you like me now as you did when we met; did I turn out to be someone you regret?

You tried to shape me, body and soul; to make me into your vision was your goal.

I am what I am, and that's no shame; the one you met at the football game.

Don't do any of your rearranging; I'm not a baby that needs changing.

Let's accept each other with our little quirks, let's fight the devil wherever he lurks

Together we can lighten up our load as we skip down the yellow brick road.

Make light of our troubles, and double our fun, the two of us living as one.

We will be happy, and really sane, just as we were at the football game.

FLYING THROUGH WIND AND RAIN

Flying through wind and rain, deep into clouds and out again.

How'd I wind up doing this? Terra Firma I surely miss.

When I left, the weather was sunny, but high up here it ain't funny.

I'm flying away from the life I led; got kicked out of my nice warm bed.

The wife said leave, "I've had enough; on my nerves you got too tough."

"You're not the man I met at first; you've turned into the very worst.

The crazy things that you do now, puts a strain on our wedding vow.

You drink the booze and play with women, this marriage game you're not a winnin".

She gave me a ticket for a plane, told me not to come back again.

She handed my coat and suitcase too, then the front door she pushed me through.

She made sure I'd never be around; out of her life and out of her town.

She sent me back to my old city leaving her sitting mighty pretty.

I lost the furniture and the car so shiny: I was thrown out on my hiney

The house was hers, so the law said, made me so mad, I saw red.

Guess I got just what I deserved 'cuz I broke the promised word.

I never thought I'd turn out to be, the one to cause such misery.

Now here I am in a stormy sky; too scared to shake and too dry to cry.

Flying through wind and rain; deep into clouds and out again.

The moral of this tale of sorrow and woe; you shall reap the things that you sow!

TOILET SEAT

A toilet seat can be contentious, devastating and pretentious.

It can cause a lot of strife, with a man and his wife.

In many a talk it comes up, about the seat being down or up.

But things just don't seem to balance, as most men keep their silence.

You don't hear us a bitchin', nor a fit are we a pitchin'.

We don't make a nasty sound, when she leaves th' damn seat down.

Now what I keep a thinkin', it's not fair and it's a stinkin'.

If it's dark and I don't see, and upon that seat I do pee,

and she sits down on my wetness, I better be in running fitness.

I'd never hear the end of it, my peein' there I'd need to quit.

If I don't put that seat back down like she thinks I outta'.

She says her butt will fall right thru into that cold cold water.

Why can't she look where her sittin' is, like I should look before I whizz.

When a man was first created, how did he get to be more obligated,
in the way of manly missions, to return the seat, to the down position?
What I'd really like to know, which way should the seat rule go?
Why shouldn't the woman be the one, to put the seat back up when she is done?

BOOK NINE

Seniors

THAT SPECIAL PLACE

OH BLOOD OF MINE

I am diabetic, sometimes my blood sugar levels are on a roller coaster ride, consequently, I check it often. Poking my fingers with a small needle and placing blood on a test strip that is attached to a meter and logging the results.

I've pretty well become accustomed to it, however, it can be a pain (pun intended) at times. I'm a firm believer that when one is stuck with lemons, make lemonade.

So, I re-wrote one of Johnny Cash's hit songs to express my experience with diabetes. The song is "I WALK THE LINE', so think of the below poem in that tune.

OH BLOOD OF MINE

By Adrian Ray Evans.. (Remember now, to
the tune of "I Walk the line")

I keep a close watch on this blood of mine
Because you're mine, I walk the line.
I keep my fingers wide open all the time
I keep the ends out for the needle that shines
Because you're fine, oh blood of mine.
I find it very very easy to be blue
Cause I stick my finger when each day is through.
Yes I'll admit that I'm a fool for you

Because you're fine, Oh blood of mine.
As sure as night is dark and day is light
I keep you in my veins both day and night
And happiness I've known proves that it's right
Because you're fine, oh blood of mine.
You've got a way to keep me on your side
You give me cause for love that I can't hide
For you I know I'd even try to turn the tide.
Because you're fine, oh blood of mine.
I keep a close watch on this blood of mine
Because you're mine, I walk the line.
I keep my fingers wide open all the time
I keep the ends out for the needle that shines
Because you're fine, oh blood of mine.

SMILEY GRIN

If I have my way about this day, I'll make it a smiley one.

I'll have some fun while doing the things that needs to be done.

My body can't jump but my mind can skip, I'm too old for a backward flip.

My head is bald and my sick feet tingle, I'm so broke my pockets don't jingle.

But I feel really blessed, for what little health I have left.

I can still talk and see a bit, and my brain still has some wit.

Age has made me a little overweight; I can salute the flag and stand up straight,

When it comes to pains, I have many, but not if I take my pills a plenty.

There're shots for this and shots for that, so many shots, my butt won't sat.

I go to bed as the sun goes down, that's not me out runnin' round.

But when I'm awake during the day, my heart is joyous and wants to play.

You won't hear me go boo-hoo, not if I can get a nap or two.

I can snooze in any chair, I can snooze right here or over there.

So why on earth would I complain, I'm sleeping like a little baby again?

So paint my face with a smiley grin, I'm in pretty good shape for the shape I'm in.

SOLITARY

I once had a TV addiction; I'd watch anything, even fiction.
I'd watch the news, cartoons and soaps, and all those old movies for senile dopes.
    I don't know how long I would sit, while glued to the screen there in front of it.
    If I sat far back the words I couldn't hear, but if I moved close, my sight would veer.
So I decided I'd go fishin' for a different stupid addiction.
I turned to my computer and ask this question:. Please computer, gimme a new direction.
    We all know what a computer will do; it doesn't give a damn about you.
    It'll just spit out its own info, if it fits you it'll make you glow.
But if it doesn't and it goes bum, it'll probably cost you a tidy sum.
If not money or personnel stuff, the cost can still be mighty tough.
    Now this machine has me playing a game, I'm real sure I'll not be the same.
    I'm here playing it both day and night, no matter the weather, cloudy or bright.

The wife says I'm becoming a stranger, does that mean
I'm in marriage danger?
Sometimes I think I'll go back to TV, before this game
makes a wreck of me.
    Sometimes I feel like doing hara-kiri,
    Because of this game called soli-a-tarie.

FIXED INCOME

Go through your wardrobe, and check out the fit, there might be some clothes you will need to git.

If there's an up-coming special affair, some of that old stuff, you can't wear.

Those quick years will pass you by; your changing body will make you cry.

I got out a shirt, and it was still white; around the collar, it was kinda' tight.

I tried to button it for a tie, it wouldn't button I didn't know why.

That shirt now had a shrunken collar, so damn small, I could hardly swaller.

It turned out to be a sad situation; around my neck a choking invitation.

But that my friend wasn't the half of it, when I tried the suit, it no longer fit.

The waist had shrunk the crotch got smaller and even the legs had gotten taller.

That suit wasn't made for me; it was for the one I used to be.

I had to pay a visit to the clothing store, to replace the clothes that didn't fit no more.

I was shocked at what the store clerk said; it frustrated me and I saw red.

He said "Sir, the price is higher; up from when you were a younger buyer!"

He quoted me a tidy sum, too much for a dude on a fixed income.

So a tailor I went to see,.. to make that suit fit to me.

That greedy tailor, he wanted more than the man over at the clothing store.

So back to the house to see what I could do; I got out some thread and a needle, too.

I cut and sewed and did some patchin', I put some room where room was lackin'.

Then my wife came to the scene; she got so sick her face turned green.

She said, "Lord o'mighty, what've you done?. You look like a clown dressed for fun."

She said we were going to a serious event, so back to the clothing store I went.

I bought a suit, shirt and tie; that damn bill made me cry.

From now on I'll have a real tight fist; squeeze a nickel and make it twist,

I can't spend another tidy sum, because I'm a man on a fixed income.

COLONOSCOPY

'Sted of out fishin 'where you ought to be, you're lying on a bed after a colonoscopy.

A colonoscopy sure is a breeze; roll on your side and say, "Stick it to me please."

They'll shove that thing up your butt, you won't see 'cuz your eyes are shut.

The doc will check on your insides and print them on some picture slides.

Now the secret for it not to hurt, get knocked out, don't be alert.

But getting prepared is a different story; you'll sit on the throne in all your glory.

After you drink that awful stuff' you'll be too weak to be tough.

As you're coming awake, there in your bed, rubbin' your belly and scratching your head,

You'll try real hard to have some class, holding back and not pass gas.

But let all go my good friend; don't try hard to be a gentleman.

Those around you know for sure, that bloated gas you must endure.

So blow if you must and feel free, everyone does, after a colonoscopy.

OPEN YOUR HEART

A reflection on my open heart surgery in August of 2012

Open your heart is a tricky phrase; it could mean kindness and charity,
But in my case, it turned out to be an operation of heart surgery.
They carved a split in my chest, and broke the bone in my breast.
They put their hands inside my bod and around my heart, they did prod.
They tackled a real tough chore, blood wasn't flowing right anymorc.
While fixing me they couldn't blunder, or I'd wind up six feet under.
Did it bother me? Oh heck no, fast asleep they made me go.
My head didn't move my knee didn't jerk; I stayed still so they could work.
I felt no pain, not at all; they knocked me out with propafol.
The drug that made too much action and did in that Michel Jackson.
But I was much safer than he because a pro gave the drug to me.

They sewed me up and sent me away, so my heart could pump another day.

Now those faithful servants I do hold dear, they opened my heart and saved my rear.

BOOK TEN

Compassion

This book is dedicated to those who have family in home care and nursing homes.

WINTER SUNDOWN

SECOND CHILDHOOD

My momma washed my butt, changed my diaper and fed me with a spoon.

She rocked me to sleep and gently placed me in my crib, there in her own bedroom.

Alone I was never, and cold I did not feel, 'cuz she kept me covered from head to heel.

If I'd wake during the night, be I sick or just in fright,

She'd quickly arise to any occasion, being at my call was an easy decision.

She'd sing a tune in a low soft voice bringing me comfort was her very first choice.

Now I don't remember those early days, I was far too young and not set in my ways

She was always there for me until I was grown and even then I'd seek her out if I felt alone.

Now Momma is old and the table has turned.. It's time for me to use the things I've learned.

By her side I'll try to be, to care for Momma like she cared for me.

To wash her body and soothe her woes, do her laundry and change her clothes.

Put her to sleep in her nice warm bed, fluff her pillow and place her head.

Be ready to sing with soft glory, kiss her goodnight and tell her a story.

She may not remember the things I've done, but neither did I when I was young.

When I was not set in my way; when I cried all night and slept all day.

Now Momma is old and her ways are set, on my nerves she will sometimes get.

Just like I often did; back when I was a kid.

Quite often the child in me was not so good, now its Momma's turn in her second childhood.

NURSING HOME

Little old lady, sitting in her bed, shoulders humped to the back of her head.

Life goes on day after day, no place to go no place to play.

Sometimes she will know you sometimes she don't, sometimes she'll talk sometimes she won't.

Her body is slipping day by day, her mind is losing and fading away.

The nurses come to fix her aches and pains with shots and pills and pillows and things.

But what they can't fix is deep in her head, she wants to go home to her own warm bed.

She wants to be back in her lively youth, her mind can't grasp the aging truth.

She longs for the day she will be whole again, completely in charge and wearing a grin.

What we don't tell her and she don't see is back in her bed she'll never be.

In this place she will long remain, never to go home--ever again.

So if your someone is stuck in a space, whether it is home or a nursing place,

Go see them often and bring them joy, be it an old lady or a sick little boy.

Don't let them be forgotten, lonely and distraught, bring them company, laughter and thought.
Bring them a card or a flower or two and say to them, I really, really do love you.
And as you head to her room down the hall past other old folks, wave to them all.
Always be happy and never aloof, let your smile be facial proof,
That you're here and they're not alone,

as life goes on in a nursing home.

BEDSIDE VIGIL

It isn't easy, saying what you want to say when you know a loved one is passing away.

Sitting around the death bedside, some of us stared, some of us cried.

There's no measuring the way some think, some of us show it some just can't.

If our emotions were on our sleeve, all would know how sad we grieve.

Those whose feelings they tend to hide are all torn up, deep inside.

Those who cry and have a fit, will much sooner get over it.

Releasing that pressure that is inward gets us moving easier onward.

Time goes slow but yet is fleeting, to be there when a heart stops beating.

To see a slight smile on a passing face, you know they're going to a better place.

It was nice to have them here but now they're a memory to hold dear.

Hang their picture where all can see and save a piece of their memory.

They're not sad, don't you know, they knew it was their time to go.

If you believe that somehow they're looking down upon you now

Then you know, they're content, for you were there when they went.

Though their body was working little, their brain knew of your bedside vigil.

A LOVED ONE, GOOD BYE

DOROTHY'S LIGHTHOUSE

In January of 1997, my Mother-in-law, Dorothy Kirk, sent me a birthday card with the above picture.

I did a 24 x 30 oil painting of it on canvas.. The poem below is dedicated to her memory.

She passed November 13th 2014.

It isn't easy, saying what you want to say when you know a loved one is passing away.

You know the words, but just can't say it; you try real hard, but can't even pray it.

You have this feeling inside of you. No matter how you say it, it doesn't sound true.

It just doesn't express the way you've felt about this hand, you've just been dealt.

That's when it's time to stop, and take a breath. You're not alone with this loved one's death.

The world doesn't revolve around your face; there're other mourners in this sad place.

They may need you to be there for them as their loved one's eyes are growing dim.

As you watch a loved one's very last breath, think of all the peace in their death.

No more pain, no more strife, think of the good things in their life.

No matter where their beliefs may take them, our loving memories won't forsake them.

Some folks say it's not good-by, it's just farewell, so try not to cry.

We had them around, and that was good; they helped our emotional livelihood.

Now let's turn to one another; sister to sister and brother to brother.

Let's rejoice in our sorrow and move on to a bright tomorrow.

Be glad you loved them and did not wait,

to say. "I love you" before it was too late.

GRIEF LIKE A WEED

Lost loves and lost love lives causes grief and much' much strife.

Sometimes the pain won't go away; it just lingers, day after day.

It stings like a needle in the heart, tearing your emotions completely apart.

It sucks the blood from your brain; your head is spinning, like a circling drain.

Some days you're as low as low low dirt; you've lost a loved one, and you feel the hurt,

Then on the days you're feeling great you want to sing, but you hesitate.

You feel guilty for being joyful, and then you go back to feeling awful.

It's your duty; you're sure as can be, to live your life in misery.

Now if you listen and listen clear, a voice might whisper in your ear.

That voice will tell you "Don't be sad, think of the good times we have had."

That voice will sooth you if you'll let it, then the serenity, you will get it.

If your loved one could speak from the grave, they'd tell you to grief, don't be a slave.

Now if you confide in counsel that's witty, they'll suggest it's just self pity.

You and I know that's just not true 'cause we and they, don't wear the same shoe.

They just say that grief is a seed, which grows and grows into a weed.

And just like a weed, if you nourish it, that grief will grow and never quit

Now if you want to lose that weed of grief, pull it out by the roots and stomp on it.

Replace it with your love's favorite flower, one that will give smiles, hour after hour.

Now don't you ever, ever forget, grief like a weed is not a good fit.

And grief like a weed, as you know, with nourishment it will grow.

CLOSING WINDOW

Based on a dream I had about my passing

WINDOWS

The twilight is coming down; the end is near. From not far away, I can vaguely hear,

a voice is beckoning oh so softly, "Come, my friend, come walk with me."

Is this the voice of my inner self calling me to a golden wealth?

The wealth of peace no pain no worry, going slow while in no hurry?

You knew this path would come your way, on this earth you can no longer stay.

You've paid for your sins repeatedly, now rest in peace for eternity.

To dust your body surely will go but your memory will grow and grow.

You changed your ways before it was too late; you've painted your own huge golden gate.

You've showed the world there is hope for those who've lived with wine and dope.

Be at peace that your legacy is living a life of sobriety.

As the window closes and the lights go down, don't fade away with a solemn frown.

Chest out, belly back, head up, chin in; go out of this world with a big wide grin.

In your own little way, you're leaving it better for all today.

Your exit, don't be opposing; praise your life as your window is closing.

I- Z–THE- END

Now you've reached the end of my stories in their splendor and all their glories.

You were warned on the very first page, that with my views you would engage.

You were not asked to agree but if you did, it's because you see

Some of my points were worth taking to deeper thoughts and insight making.

This world can be a better place if we all wear a real good face.

A large smile or just a grin to show the hope we have within.

Just praying for peace isn't going to get it; we need to do more than just let it.

Do something that will build a bond, for right now and well beyond.

Raise all hopes in everyone that shedding blood is not how it's done.

At a table of peace we should sit, so all worldly folks harmoniously fit.

No partiality should there be with race or creed or nationality.

In this life your place is earned, not by color but by work confirmed.

Let's not force or even try, to instill our ways on the other guy.

If he likes the way we do it he will soon come around to it.

Let's just show him the good in us, so he'll jump on our freedom bus.

No shootin', stabbin', robbin' or killin', just all join hands when we're willin'.

This may be the end of this manuscript, but not the end of this pragmatist.

Wanting to spread peace and knock out sin, only when that's done.... will I- Z–the- END .

(Z, as in the end of the alphabet and the end of this manuscript))

THE END

BUTTERFLIES TWO

Appendix

ILLUSTRATIONS

(Photo copies of original oil paintings by Adrian Ray Evans)

MORNING AFTER	33 x 39 oil on canvas and board
GRANNIE'S HOBBY	16 x 20 oil on canvas
MOM'S TABLE	24 x 36 oil on board
ONE NATION	48 x 60 oil on gallery-wrap board
BLESSED TIMES	33 x 48 oil on board
LITTLE PEOPLE PAINTER	12 x 16 oil on canvas board
JUNIORS SUNSET	16 x 20 oil on canvas
WARP SPEED	36 x 48 oil on board
THE SEASON	18 x 24 oil on gallery-wrap board
HURRICANE HAPPENING	20 x 34 oil on board
EVIL	24 x 36 oil on gallery-wrap board
LEVITATION	18 x 24 oil on canvas
THAT SPECIAL PLACE	48 x 60 oil on gallery-wrap board

WINTER SUNDOWN	16 x 20 oil on canvas board
DOROTHY'S LIGHTHOUSE	24 x 30 Oil on canvas
WINDOWS	36 x 48 oil on gallery-wrap board
BUTTERFLIES TWO	16 x 20 oil on board

Review Requested:

If you loved this book, would you please provide a review at Amazon.com?

CPSIA information can be obtained
at www.ICGtesting.com
Printed in the USA
FFOW03n1909071215
19189FF